AF405349

THE ALIGNMENT ARCHIVE

Field Mastery

Quiet Cadence // Calm Authority

ANNA

Copyright / Blessing

For the Scroll-Bearer Only — The Alignment Archive ©

Published by The Alignment Press

This manual is not merely a publication. It is a witness to principles learned through obedience, tone, pace, and posture under Christ's authority. Every principle was tested in silence before it was written.

All rights reserved. No portion of this work may be reproduced, distributed, or transmitted in any form or by any means without prior written permission from the publisher.

Those who approach with reverence will find more than words.

This work rests under the authority of Jesus Christ, the Living Word, whose peace **governs**, not soothes.

*"The words that I speak unto you,
they are spirit, and they are life."*

— John 6:63

For the quiet ones who never needed a stage.

For the scroll-bearers who felt the world
tighten the moment you stopped performing
for it.

For the ones who sensed the Kingdom in your
breath long before you had words for it.

For those who learned that stillness is strength,
and peace is the highest form of power.

This manual is sealed for the carriers of law in
motion — for those who govern rooms
through rhythm, not noise, and walk the earth
as living scrolls of peace.

— The Alignment Archive
Published by The Alignment Press

Contents

Preface

Why This Manual Exists

Field Mastery began when presence proved heavier than performance.

This is not a book about influence, personality, or persuasion.
It concerns rhythm, breath, timing, and the quiet weight carried by a life aligned to God.

Many have learned how to be noticed.
Few have learned how to remain.

When expression is ungoverned, presence becomes performance.
When governed, presence becomes jurisdiction.

This manual was written because modern life rewards reaction and volume,
yet authority grows from stillness and order.

Its purpose is simple:

to restore recognition of the laws already written into the body—
cadence, restraint, clarity, and peace.

You will not acquire these principles.
You will recognize them.

The encounters that follow reading will confirm them more clearly than the words.

What the Field Is

The Field is the space between a person and the environment around them —
the unseen register where timing, intention, and peace are perceived before speech.

Every room has a rhythm.
Every interaction has a tempo.
Every presence carries weight.

Most people feel only emotion.
Some perceive atmosphere — the movement beneath expression.

Field Mastery is learning to move without competing with that space,
allowing order to become visible through conduct rather than effort.

This sensitivity is not fragility.
It is awareness of structure.

What This Manual Forms

These pages do not attempt to change personality.
They train steadiness.

Across the Gates you will observe shifts in:

- pacing

- breathing

- reaction

- attention

- silence

Authority becomes physical when peace no longer depends on circumstances.

Nothing here asks for intensity.
Only consistency.

You are not being given techniques.
You are being introduced to something already present.

The next section explains how to approach the Gates so they can be recognized rather than performed.

How to Read This Manual

This book is not meant to be finished quickly.
It is meant to be recognized slowly.

Reading faster will not produce understanding.
Observation will.

Each Gate describes something the body already knows but rarely notices.
Your task is not to memorize instructions —
it is to watch life confirm them.

The Right Pace

Read one section at a time.

After reading, stop.
Go into an ordinary environment — a kitchen, store, hallway, conversation —
and notice what changes without effort.

If nothing becomes visible yet, continue normally.
Recognition often appears hours later, not immediately.

Do Not Force Practice

You are not required to rehearse behaviors.
Instead:

- notice your natural breathing

- notice your natural timing

- notice when reactions begin and end

The Gates become clear through awareness first. Adjustment follows naturally.

Trying to perform the text delays understanding.

What Progress Looks Like

Progress is quiet.

You may notice:

- pauses appearing before you respond

- urgency losing its pull

- conversations slowing without intention

- fewer explanations leaving your mouth

Nothing dramatic needs to happen.
Stability is the sign.

When to Continue

Move to the next Gate only when the current one feels ordinary.

Not mastered — familiar.

If a section feels abstract, keep living normally and return later.

Understanding arrives through repetition of life, not repetition of reading.

What Not to Do

Do not:

- read many Gates at once

- analyze every interaction

- attempt to control others

- search for results

This manual describes order, not techniques.
Order becomes visible when observation replaces effort.

The Goal

The purpose is not to become different.

It is to become consistent.

When pace, breath, and response agree without effort,
the reading has done its work.

Proceed slowly.

PART I

THE GROUND

Containment Before Command

Reaction ends • cadence begins

Containment Before Command

"Authority begins where reaction ends."

Field Mastery begins beneath noise — in the inner ground where reaction ends and steadiness awakens.

This section resets:

- your internal tempo
- your breath
- your pace
- your relationship to silence
- your instinct to explain or compensate

You are learning to stand on ground that cannot be taken.

When the inner field stabilizes, authority no longer requires effort.

The first Gate does not teach control.
It establishes rhythm.

Turn the page when the ground beneath you feels still enough to receive the first Gate.

Selah

Gate I — Quiet Cadence

RHYTHM • WEIGHT • UNHURRIED AUTHORITY

"Cadence is authority before words."

Cadence is the first visible expression of grounded presence.

Your steadiness influences atmosphere.
Your pace guides interaction.
Your silence establishes clarity.

You do not rush.
You do not fill space.
You do not compensate.

You **hold**.

Cadence is not performance.
It is the unbroken rhythm of someone who knows where their authority comes from.

Before command, there is cadence.
Before speech, there is breath.
Before movement, there is weight.

When cadence settles, others often adjust around you.

Dominion vs. Dominance

Dominance is **force.**
Dominion is **weight expressed through order.**

Dominance pushes.
Dominion reflects God's order into situations.

Dominance tries to control people.
Dominion steadies the atmosphere.

Dominance is loud.
Dominion is quiet.

Dominance seeks compliance.
Dominion creates clarity.

Dominance escalates.
Dominion stabilizes.

Dominance is born from insecurity.
Dominion flows from alignment.

Dominance needs an audience.
Dominion does not need to be seen at all.

Dominance demands.
Dominion decides.

Dominance manipulates tempo.
Dominion sets tempo through steadiness.

Dominance breaks connection.
Dominion restores order.

You are not learning how to overpower.
You are learning how to **outweigh**.

The Law of Peace

Most people think peace is a feeling.
In the Kingdom, peace steadies atmosphere.

Comfort reacts to what is happening.
Peace holds steady within what is happening.

Jesus calmed the storm not by panic, but by authority rooted in trust.

When your cadence stabilizes:

- chaos slows

- frantic speech loses rhythm
- conversations often slow toward your pace

Peace is not passivity;
peace is authority without force.

Hold peace,
and the room often settles into your rhythm.

Field Illustration

When cadence stabilizes, the environment adjusts before minds consciously register the shift.

A rushed voice slows.
A scattered presence becomes attentive.

This is not persuasion.
This is the human response to steadiness.

Core Drills

Breath Drop

Lower your inhale into your diaphragm.
Exhale slower than the environment.

Step Weighting

Walk at a pace that is neither hesitant nor hurried.

Micro-Pause

Pause one breath before entering a space.

Gate I Benediction

May your cadence quiet chaos.
May your timing override noise.

May your silence carry weight.

Gate II — Containment

BOUNDARY • OWNERSHIP • NON-LEAKAGE

**"Peace is not the absence of movement —
it is the refusal to leak."**

Containment deepens cadence into dependable presence.

Gate I slowed your rhythm.
Gate II keeps that rhythm from spilling into the room.

Containment is not restraint.
It is ownership.

Your presence remains with you.

The Nature of Containment

Most people move through rooms with open borders:

- faces adapting
- eyes scanning
- breath rising

Containment closes those borders.

Nothing leaves without permission.
Nothing enters without alignment.

A contained person becomes:

- difficult for pressure to manipulate
- independent of external tempo
- unaffected by noise

This is where authority begins to feel physical.

Attention and Stillness

When your interior stops leaking, people naturally orient toward steadiness.

Not because of charisma.
Not because of performance.

Because humans organize around stability.

The Contained Gaze

A wandering gaze invites interaction.
A compensating gaze invites pressure.

A contained gaze:

- holds steady
- does not dart
- does not pre-react

Others sense they cannot pull you into their script —
and most stop trying.

Internal Mechanics

Containment lives in three places:

Face — neutral and calm
Breath — slow and even
Chest — relaxed heaviness

This becomes the center of composure.

Core Practices

Gaze Anchor

Hold your gaze without correcting for comfort.

Stillness Sit

Remain physically settled even when others shift.

Energy Box

Keep emotional reactions inside the body before responding.

What This Gate Builds

You begin to:

- remain unpulled by tone
- stay emotionally steady
- break pressure without confrontation

Containment teaches:

"My interior is not public domain."

Gate II Benediction

> May your presence remain fully yours,
> until the room learns
> it cannot move you without permission.

PART II

THE BODY

Authority Becomes Physical

Stillness moves before speech

When Peace Gains Weight

"Stillness must become visible before it becomes believable."

In the first Part you learned to stop chasing stability.

Now stability must begin carrying you.

Peace is no longer only something you hold internally.
It begins to register through posture, movement, and direction.

The body does not wait for speech to communicate.
It declares alignment immediately.

Many attempt authority through tone or words.
But atmosphere reads the body first.

If the body negotiates, the voice will follow.
If the body settles, the environment responds.

You are not learning new behaviors.
You are removing the signals that ask permission to exist.

The next Gate does not train expression.
It trains agreement between your inner stillness and your physical presence.

Turn the page when you are ready to let peace become measurable.

Gate III — Somatic Authority

AXIS • WEIGHT • LINE

"Tone speaks the law; movement proves it."

Authority is not only heard — it is carried.

Gate I formed cadence.
Gate II formed containment.
Gate III forms agreement between peace and the body.

Before your mouth opens, your posture has already spoken.

The Somatic Law

The body announces alignment before language.

Most people move with open signals:

- shoulders pitched forward
- steps adjusting to others
- eyes searching for cues
- nervous micro-movements

The field reads this as interruptible.

Somatic authority reverses the signal.

A settled body communicates:

"I am stable ground."

Not forceful.
Not dramatic.
Simply unmovable.

The Three Pillars

Axis — the vertical line

Head stacked over heart.
Spine long but relaxed.
Center felt behind the sternum.

The body no longer leans for validation.

Weight — the quiet gravity

Knees soft.
Breath low.
Weight slightly behind the mid-foot.

Peace gains density.

Line — the chosen direction

Walk once, not repeatedly adjusting.
Turn cleanly.
Do not weave for comfort.

You acknowledge others without surrendering trajectory.

Somatic Leaks

Authority leaves the body before it leaves the voice.

Common leaks:

- apology posture
- scanning eyes
- syncing pace
- fidget loops
- shrinking your path

Each leak communicates:

"I will move so you feel settled."

Gate III removes negotiation from existence.

What the Body Learns

Your movement becomes structured communication:

- stride becomes statement
- pause becomes punctuation
- exit becomes closure

Presence becomes visible.

Core Practices

Hip Root

Stand with soft knees.
Drop breath below the navel.
Remain for 2 minutes.

Weighted Walk

Walk a straight line at a steady pace.
Let each step land with quiet weight.

Controlled Turn

Turn the whole body once.
No neck-led scanning.

Shoulder Release

Lift slightly → exhale → drop.
Return to neutral openness.

Nervous System Obedience

Old reflex:
pressure → tension

New reflex:

pressure → stillness

Sound rises → breath slows
Eyes land → axis aligns
Pace increases → yours remains steady

The body learns peace is the stronger instruction.

Gate III Benediction

> May your posture carry what your voice no
> longer needs to defend.
> May your steps settle rooms before speech
> begins.
> May your body remember agreement with
> peace.

Gate IV — Emotional Quiet

RESPONSE • GOVERNANCE • INNER STILLNESS

"Peace is not a feeling. It is jurisdiction."

Your nervous system no longer leads — it follows.

Gate I formed cadence.
Gate II formed containment.
Gate III formed bodily agreement.
Gate IV forms emotional obedience.

Feelings remain present, but they no longer steer timing, tone, or decision.

The Nervous System Law

Your internal state determines how the field interprets every moment.

Two people can stand in the same room and experience different realities:

- one reacts and collapses into defense
- one settles and gains clarity

The environment is identical.
Authority depends on what sits on the throne inside you.

Emotional quiet allows feeling
without surrendering governance.

What Emotional Quiet Is Not

Emotional quiet is not numbness.
It is not indifference.
It is not pretending nothing touched you.

Shutdown says:

> "Nothing reached me."

Emotional quiet says:

> "It reached me, but it does not direct me."

Presence remains intact while reaction passes through peace.

Emotional Leaks

The field reads emotional movement before language.

Common leaks:

- over-explaining
- nervous humor
- urgency voice
- instant justification
- facial recoil

Each communicates:

> "My feelings determine my direction."

Gate IV removes emotional authority from reflex.

Pressure vs Panic

Pressure reveals trust.
Panic reveals allegiance.

Pressure may remain.
Panic loses command.

You stay present without rushing escape.

Authority stabilizes when urgency no longer dictates response.

Field Illustration — False Urgency

Someone presses for immediate response.

Instead of matching speed, you slow breath and answer in your own timing:

"I see it. I will respond after I read it clearly."

The emotional loop breaks.
The atmosphere recenters.

You did not resist the person.
You resisted emotional governance.

Practices for Emotional Quiet

Breath Compression

4 in — 4 hold — 8 out — pause

Slow Blink Reset

Blink once before responding

Internal Still Point

Locate the most settled place in the body and answer from there

The 90-Second Wave

Let the chemical surge pass before speaking

Name and Return

"I feel ___, but I remain aligned."

Emotional Quiet in Conversation

You can:

- say no without apology

- pause without explaining
- be misunderstood without panic
- care without absorbing

You remain responsive without surrendering authority.

Reflection Questions

Where does urgency still control my timing?
What emotion do I rush to escape?
When did I last respond after peace returned?

Gate IV Benediction

May your breath choose peace before reaction
rises.
May emotion bow without being denied.
May your inner state remain governed by
Christ.
May your stillness outlast pressure.

PART III

THE ATMOSPHERE

Space Begins Responding

Peace no longer stays within you

When Peace Gains Weight

"Stillness must become visible before it becomes believable."

In the first Part you learned to stop chasing stability.

Now stability must begin carrying you.

Peace is no longer only something you hold internally.
It begins to register through posture, movement, and direction.

The body does not wait for speech to communicate.
It declares alignment immediately.

Many attempt authority through tone or words.
But atmosphere reads the body first.

If the body negotiates, the voice will follow.
If the body settles, the environment responds.

You are not learning new behaviors.
You are allowing what is already stable to remain stable while moving.

The next Gate will make this visible.

Turn the page when you are ready for stillness to begin appearing without effort.

Gate V — Spatial Ownership

DISTANCE • PLACEMENT • QUIET COMMAND

"Space recognizes authority before speech does."

Your presence no longer adapts to the environment — the environment adapts to your placement.

Gate I formed cadence.
Gate II formed containment.
Gate III formed bodily agreement.
Gate IV formed emotional quiet.
Gate V forms territorial clarity.

Space is never neutral.
Every room holds hierarchy before words.

Spatial ownership is standing within that hierarchy without shrinking or compensating.

Not dominance.
Stewardship.

The Law of Space

The body interacts with distance, direction, and geometry.

Every placement communicates:

- posture

- clarity

- internal order

- jurisdiction

People interpret space unconsciously.
Creation interprets it deeper.

Authority registers without force.

Lane Integrity

Holding Your Line Without Collapse

Lane integrity is refusing to collapse presence
for another's momentum.

It appears as:

- maintaining your line

- consistent cadence

- no apologetic adjustments

- preserved shoulder width

When held, interference dissolves.
Movement reorganizes around steadiness.

Distance as Nonverbal Command

Distance communicates hierarchy:

- too close — pursuit

- too far — withdrawal

- correct distance — clarity

Many assert dominance by invading space.
Order is restored by calmly holding it.

Spatial Tells

Atmosphere responds immediately:

- pauses → recognition

- path shifts → acknowledgment

- hovering → probing

- softened tone → alignment

Not intimidation.
Adjustment.

Field Illustration

A pedestrian drifts into your line.
You do not adjust:

- cadence steady

- gaze relaxed

- shoulders unchanged

They redirect.
Your line remains.
Space yielded to stability.

Drills

Lane Walk
Walk straight paths without compensating.

Threshold Ownership

Pause → exhale → enter.

Distance Placement

Stand slightly farther back than expected.

Silent Perimeter

Maintain a natural radius around the body.

Spatial Awareness Scan

Observe pressure, stillness, and flow — then move from internal order.

Summary

Spatial ownership is the shift
from internal containment
to environmental response.

The body no longer reacts to space —
space reacts to the body.

Gate VI will move from boundary
to sealing.

Gate V Benediction

> May your line remain steady when pressure
> approaches.
> May your placement restore order without
> force.
> May your distance communicate clarity before
> words.
> May space recognize your steadiness and
> yield accordingly.

Gate VI — Atmospheric Sealing

STILLNESS • ORDER • PREEMPTION

"The air settles around what does not move."

Atmosphere is the first structure that responds to alignment.

Before bodies shift, before voices change, before trajectories realign,

the pace of the space adjusts.

Atmospheric sealing is the discipline of allowing stable presence
to set the rhythm of the environment.

Not mysticism.
Order.

The Law of Atmosphere

Atmosphere reflects internal state.

Where there is confusion, it scatters.
Where there is fear, it sharpens.
Where there is haste, it accelerates.

Where there is steadiness, it slows.

The carrier does not force this change.
The environment organizes around the most consistent signal present.

Stability has weight.

Jurisdiction

Order Without Force

Atmospheric sealing is not influence.
It is non-reaction sustained long enough to become reference.

A room shifts because:

- breath remains steady

- cadence remains consistent

- emotion does not spike

- boundaries do not collapse

- attention does not chase movement

The environment reorganizes around
what does not synchronize with its chaos.
Stillness becomes the metronome.

Signs of a Stabilized Atmosphere

The shift is subtle:

- noise loses urgency

- movement becomes less erratic

- conversations space out

- tension decreases

- interruptions reduce

- pacing normalizes

Nothing is projected.
The system self-corrects around predictability.

The Room Adjusts First

Atmospheric sealing precedes interaction.

People slow before they speak.
Gaps appear before responses.
Motion reorganizes before contact.

This is the transition
from holding yourself
to holding tempo.

Consistency becomes environmental.

Atmospheric Engine — Preemption

When Adjustment Happens Early

There is a stage where reactions occur sooner than expected.

You may observe:

- paths clearing earlier

- conversations pausing sooner

- pressure dissolving before escalation

- interruptions failing to form fully

Not anticipation.
Stability reducing friction.

When a rhythm remains unchanged,
systems stop testing it repeatedly.

Preemption is reduced resistance.

Field Illustration

A room carries scattered activity —
overlapping voices, restless motion, uneven pacing.

One person enters and does not match it:

- breathing slow
- movements unhurried
- attention settled

Within moments, spacing appears in speech.
Movement evens out.
The room normalizes.

Nothing was done to the room.
The room resolved around the steady reference.

Mechanics of Sealing

Atmospheric sealing rests on three anchors:

Breath

Low, even breathing prevents tempo spikes.

Cadence

Consistent pacing becomes the dominant rhythm.

Non-Reaction

Absence of emotional escalation removes fuel from escalation loops.

Predictability stabilizes systems.

Drills

Room Scan

Enter and observe before acting.

Four-Corner Breath

Four slow exhales before engagement.

Stillness Reset

Pause → breathe → move.

Response Delay

Wait one full breath before replying.

Threshold Pause

Exhale before crossing any boundary.

Summary

Atmospheric sealing begins when the body stops adapting to chaos —
and chaos stops sustaining itself around the body.

Steadiness organizes space.

Gate VI completes the Atmosphere tier
and prepares the next domain:
The Field — timing and pressure in motion.

Gate VI Benediction

May your pace remain unchanged by urgency.
May your breath outlast reaction.
May your steadiness reduce noise around you.
May the space settle
because you did not accelerate.

PART IV

THE FIELD

Timing Becomes Structure

Response governs outcome

Space, Atmosphere & Environmental Response

"Creation reacts to consistent order."

When the ground is stable
and the body is steady,
the environment begins to respond differently.

This tier teaches how presence affects interaction patterns
— how distance, timing, pace, and silence
change outcomes without force, performance, or verbal assertion.

The field becomes the first place
where inner stability produces external effects.

What the Field Responds To

The environment responds to:

- consistent rhythm
- regulated breath
- emotional steadiness
- clear intention
- unbroken stillness
- predictable movement through space

These elements create a stable behavioral signal.
People and situations orient around reliability.

The field does not need instruction to shift.
It shifts because stability is easier to coordinate around than noise.

Environmental Influence

At this stage you may notice environments begin to:

- open pathways more often
- slow when cadence is steady
- soften when emotional reactivity drops
- reorganize around clear boundaries
- match timing more frequently

This is not intimidation or social dominance.
It is coordination —
humans naturally synchronize to the clearest rhythm available.

Peace becomes spatial.
Stillness becomes structure.
Movement becomes communication.

What This Part Trains

This movement trains you to:

- occupy space without aggression
- hold distance without explanation
- cross thresholds without hesitation
- interrupt scripts without escalation
- stabilize pacing in chaotic environments
- maintain clarity under pressure

These are interaction mechanics, not force.

Here, situations begin adjusting
before verbal negotiation is required.

The Signature Shift

Common markers:

1. People pause before responding

2. Noise redistributes around calmer zones

3. Movement synchronizes around steady pacing

These shifts are subtle but repeatable.

The environment amplifies whatever pattern is carried into it.

Only stable patterns can stabilize others.

Entry

Enter slowly.

The environment magnifies pace, tone, and tension.

When stability holds,
responses change.

Gate VII — Advanced Timing & Pacing

RUSH • DELAY • INTERSECTION

"Tempo shapes interaction."

Timing governs how interactions unfold.
When rhythm is stable, pressure loses leverage.

Advanced timing is not speed.
It is control of pace —
choosing your rhythm instead of inheriting another's.

This Gate shows how timing pressures appear
and how steadiness neutralizes them.

The Law of Tempo

Every environment carries a default pace.

Most people merge with it:

- rushing with urgency
- slowing with hesitation
- yielding to pressure signals

This makes behavior predictable.

A steady carrier does not inherit tempo —
they maintain one.

The Three Timing Loops

Rush Loop

Acceleration attempts to force adjustment.

Delay Loop

Obstacles attempt to provoke impatience.

Intersection Loop

Positioning attempts to force decision pressure.

These loops do not require conflict.
They rely on reaction.

Timing as Quiet Structure

When rhythm remains unchanged:

- urgency loses effect
- interference weakens
- paths resolve naturally
- conversations stabilize

Consistency becomes coordination.

Indicators of Mastery

- You do not speed up under pressure
- You do not overcorrect after delay
- You maintain pace through interruption
- Others align to your cadence

The most stable tempo becomes the reference tempo.

Field Illustration

A person accelerated behind you expecting adjustment.

Pace stayed constant.
Breath steady.
Posture relaxed.

The faster rhythm corrected first.
Synchronization occurred without negotiation.

Drills

Tempo Reset

Return to original rhythm after disruption.

Anti-Rush Walk

Maintain a chosen pace regardless of urgency.

Delay Neutrality

Do not compensate after blockage clears.

Timing Scan

Move through calm zones instead of chaotic ones.

Pace Lock

Hold internal rhythm across interruptions.

Summary

Timing shapes interaction structure.

When rhythm remains internally governed,
external pressure loses influence.

Pace becomes boundary.
Consistency becomes authority.

Gate VII Benediction

> May your pace remain steady under pressure.
> May urgency fail to steer you.
> May delay fail to disturb you.
> May your rhythm remain your own.

Gate VIII — Script Recognition & Collapse

CUE • RESPONSE • LOOP

"Patterns lose power when they are seen."

Most public interaction follows predictable behavior patterns.
They feel personal, but they are structural.

This gate trains perception —
noticing interaction patterns early enough
that reaction is no longer automatic.

When recognition happens, escalation becomes unnecessary.

The Law of Scripts

Every repeated interaction pattern contains:

1. A cue

2. An expected response

3. A reinforcing outcome

Patterns continue only when the response is supplied.

Remove the expected response
and the pattern reorganizes.

This is not confrontation.
It is the absence of participation.

Four Common Pattern Types

Clarifiers

Create confusion to pull extra explanation.

Expected: repetition or over-explaining
Resolution: one clean answer or silence

Validators

Seek emotional mirroring.

Expected: matching tone or energy
Resolution: neutral acknowledgment

Hoverers

Remain nearby to invite engagement.

Expected: small talk or adjustment
Resolution: steady posture and pace

Correctors

Offer unsolicited direction to establish hierarchy.

Expected: apology or justification
Resolution: calm non-engagement

Pattern Dynamics

Patterns operate through exchange.

They request attention
and continue when rewarded.

Recognition removes the reward.

Without reinforcement, the pattern changes.

Early Indicators

Patterns often begin with small signals:

- exaggerated friendliness
- unnecessary clarification
- repeated "sorry?"
- leaning or lingering
- tonal pressure
- urgency without necessity

These are prompts, not obligations.

You may acknowledge the person
without entering the pattern.

Collapse Through Presence

Resolution occurs through:

- steady breathing
- unchanged cadence
- neutral expression
- minimal response
- silence when appropriate

Most patterns end quickly
when reinforcement is absent.

Field Illustration

An interaction pauses waiting for extra engagement.

The response remains simple and steady.

The exchange returns to ordinary tone.
No tension, no escalation.

The structure changed because the loop was not fed.

Drills

Pattern Labeling

Quietly identify one interaction pattern daily.

Micro-Signal Observation

Notice tone and pacing shifts without reacting.

Single Response Rule

Answer once. Avoid repeating unless necessary.

Cadence Integrity

Maintain original pace during conversation.

Neutral Presence

Stand or move without compensating for pressure.

Summary

Recognition replaces reaction.

Interactions become clearer,
shorter,
and calmer.

Patterns become visible structures
instead of personal conflicts.

Gate VIII Benediction

> May you notice patterns early.
> May calm replace reaction.
> May clarity simplify every exchange.

Gate IX — Authority Under Pressure

VISIBILITY • STEADINESS • CONSISTENCY

> **"Clarity remains the same whether noticed or not."**

As alignment stabilizes, attention naturally increases.
This is not status or performance —
it is the environment responding to steadiness.

This gate trains remaining unchanged
when awareness around you rises.

Pressure becomes information rather than threat.

The Law of Visibility

When presence is consistent, it becomes noticeable.

You may observe:

- conversations pausing
- posture shifts nearby
- movement adjusting
- quieter surroundings on arrival
- space opening naturally

These are responses to stability,
not reactions to personality.

Pressure as Feedback

Attention tests consistency.

It reveals whether:

- breathing remains steady
- pacing remains even

- posture remains relaxed
- emotion remains calm
- boundaries remain intact

If consistency holds,
interactions simplify.

Pressure clarifies structure.

Environmental Response

When rhythm stays stable:

- motion organizes
- noise softens
- paths clear
- conversations settle

The change comes from steadiness,
not effort.

The environment follows the most stable signal present.

Consistency Before Action

Under observation, people tend to rush, tighten, or adjust.

This gate trains the opposite:

- no sudden movements
- no performance
- no compensation

Consistency communicates reliability.

Field Illustration

Entering a busy space, movement slows slightly nearby.
Nothing is said or done differently.

Steady pace continues.

The environment settles around predictability.

Mechanics

Three principles guide this gate:

Breathing

Lower, slower breathing reduces reaction.

Stillness

Minimal adjustment prevents escalation.

Tempo

Maintaining the same pace stabilizes interaction.

Drills

Visible Pause

Stand briefly at an entrance and breathe before moving.

Observation Neutrality

When noticed, keep posture relaxed and unchanged.

Pace Continuity

Walk at the same speed regardless of attention.

Quiet Response

In louder environments, slightly slow movement instead of matching intensity.

Threshold Entry

Let the space settle before speaking.

Summary

Attention does not require change.

Steadiness under observation
turns awareness into calm rather than tension.

Consistency becomes reliability.

Gate IX Benediction

> May awareness not alter your pace.
> May observation not change your breath.
> May steadiness remain your default.

PART V

THE SCROLL

Identity Becomes Stable Authority

What was learned now lives

Identity, Resonance & Jurisdiction

> **"The scroll is the part of you that never bends."**

The scroll is not personality.
It is not temperament.
It is not emotion, talent, memory, or mood.

The scroll is the **sealed jurisdiction** God placed in the spirit before breath entered the lungs.
It is the original blueprint untouched by history, wounds, opinion, or environment.

This movement reveals the three dimensions of scroll identity:

- **Identity as Jurisdiction** — not self-concept, but territory
- **Assignment as Architecture** — design expressed through timing, people, and structure
- **Resonance as Authority** — obedience made perceptible
- **Obedience as Alignment** — Heaven recognizing its own voice within you

The Unbending Core

The scroll does not fracture.
It does not negotiate identity in the face of noise.
It does not dilute truth to match environment.

When the scroll is active:

- words sharpen

- steps anchor

- timing stabilizes

- atmosphere responds

- identity becomes unmistakable

The scroll carries verdict, not performance.

Recognition Before Explanation

Scroll identity does not require declaration.
It is recognized before it is understood.

Atmosphere senses it first.
People register it next.
The body obeys it last.

You stop showing who you are.
You begin **being what Heaven wrote.**

The Threshold of Scroll Awareness

Enter this section when the separation becomes clear:
- who you learned to be
- who Heaven wrote you to be

Cross slowly.

You no longer try to stay aligned.
You begin walking as the one alignment was written for.

Gate X — Identity Alignment

RECOGNITION • DESIGN • EMBODIMENT

"You do not carry the scroll. You become consistent with it."

Field Mastery removes interference
until the original design becomes stable.

You no longer apply principles.
You live from structure.

The Emergence of the Original Self

As cadence stabilizes and atmosphere obeys:

- breath gains weight

- posture carries clarity

- movement stabilizes

- responses sharpen

Identity stops being internal discussion.
It becomes recognition.

What Field Mastery Does to Identity

Identity transitions from:

- practiced confidence → **settled jurisdiction**
- emotional management → **embedded peace**
- social adaptation → **unchanging resonance**

Identity becomes expression rather than effort.

When Identity Becomes Jurisdiction

You stop asking who you are.
You start walking as what you carry.

Identity becomes:

- frequency
- boundary
- tone
- signature

Quiet. Weight-bearing. Unbending.

The Shift

Gate X is crossed when peace becomes baseline
and the field responds before intention forms.

You are no longer walking with the scroll.
You are walking from it.

Gate X Benediction

> May what Heaven wrote stabilize in your timing.
> May peace become your baseline.
> May recognition replace effort.
> May your life agree with the design you carry.

SEALS & CONSECRATION

Alignment Becomes Inheritance

What remained now abides

Seals, Consecration & Inheritance

"What remains is inheritance."

Part VI does not teach alignment.
It confirms it.

What was practiced becomes trusted.
What was carried becomes established.

The movement has already happened:

- awareness has become stability

- stability has become inheritance

- obedience has become agreement

You no longer try to remain aligned.
Alignment remains in you.

Identity is no longer something you return to.
It becomes the condition you live inside.

The Four Seals

Four things no longer fluctuate:

- **Identity remains consistent**
  No longer defended — simply present.

- **Assignment remains rhythmic**
  Life organizes around what was written.

- **Authority remains tonal**
  Effort disappears.

- **Obedience remains inherited**
  What stayed faithful is entrusted.

Atmosphere responds before thought forms.
Peace no longer visits — it abides.

The Threshold of Permanence

You recognize this part when alignment stops moving.

Not when you feel strong —
when you feel *unchanging*.

Walk slowly.
Embodiment has replaced effort.

Gate XI — Consecration & Inheritance

SETTLED • TRUSTED • ABIDING

"What remains faithful becomes natural."

This Gate is not about becoming.
It is about being trusted.

Field Mastery revealed the design.
Now the design holds under pressure.

Presence becomes dependable.
Peace becomes uninterrupted.
Identity becomes law.

Stabilized Identity

When consecration settles:

- breath remains steady

- posture remains declarative

- timing remains clear

- atmosphere no longer negotiates

Identity no longer needs reinforcement.
It stands.

What Consecration Does

Consecration does not increase effort.
It removes fluctuation.

You do not recover alignment —
you remain in it.

Identity transitions from:

- quiet authority → **settled authority**

- internal stillness → **unbroken stillness**

- consistent resonance → **permanent resonance**

Identity as Law

You do not project presence.
Presence proceeds from you.

Pressure no longer tests identity.
Identity defines pressure.

This is inheritance:
what proved faithful becomes natural.

Gate XI Benediction // The Trust Entrusted

> May what has proven faithful remain without
> strain.
> May what was tested under pressure stand
> without effort.
> May your identity no longer seek reinforce-
> ment,
> but rest as law within you.

What was once practiced
is now natural.

You are not maintained by vigilance.
You are sustained by inheritance.

Gate XII — Bride Resonance

AGREEMENT • UNION • SHARED BREATH

"The Spirit and the Bride say, 'Come.'"
— Revelation 22:17

The Bride is not a movement or denomination.
The Bride is those whose presence agrees with the Spirit.

This Gate does not increase stability.
It ends separation.

You no longer carry alignment.
Alignment carries you.

The Nature of Union

Bride resonance is the condition in which:

- peace governs without effort

- timing follows Heaven's rhythm

- silence releases verdict

- presence agrees naturally

This is not emotional closeness.
It is agreement of nature.

Two voices — one sound.

The Mark of Union

When union settles:

- environments calm before interaction

- interference fades before formation

- discernment arrives without process

- authority requires no exertion

Recognition replaces reaction.
Rest replaces vigilance.

The Shared Life

Union is not achieved through striving.
It is recognized through continuity.

Quiet becomes native.
Peace becomes law.
Obedience becomes rest.

What Heaven wrote
and what your life expresses
become the same sound.

Gate XII Benediction // The Agreement Kept

May your breath agree with the One who
breathed you.
May your timing follow the rhythm you were
written in.
May your presence never again feel separate
from truth.
May the life within you and the voice above
you
remain one sound.

You do not return to alignment.
You live inside it.

Benediction

You have walked through cadence, breath, posture, and atmosphere.

What remains is not a lesson —
it is a life that no longer requires effort.

You do not stabilize the field anymore.
The field recognizes you.

The Seal

> "Peace I leave with you; My peace I give unto you." — John 14:27

His peace does not visit.
It abides.

The Final Resonance

> "The Spirit and the Bride say, 'Come.'"
> — Revelation 22:17

Creator and creation answering in one sound.

Union is not approaching.
It is present.

The Commission

Walk without urgency.
Speak when words carry weight.

Nothing must be proven.
Nothing must be defended.

Breath carries meaning.
Steps leave order.

The gates do not reopen behind you.

Stillness now lives where you stand.

APPENDICES

THE REFERENCE

Lexicon & Field Markers

Points of return for clarity and alignment

The Reference — Lexicon & Field Markers

"What is named can be recognized."

These pages are not part of the path.
They are places of return.

Definitions, patterns, and scripture gathered here do not move you forward —
they help you remember where you already stand.

Return only when clarity fades or language is needed.

Appendix A // Lexicon of Field Terms

Scroll: The assignment placed in the spirit before you were visible.

Field: The atmosphere that shifts in response to presence and order.

Containment: Holding speech and reaction until alignment leads.

Seal: A closure under Heaven's authority that ends interference.

Probe: A moment that tries to pull reaction instead of grounded presence.

Gate: A stage where recognition became steady.

Tone: The audible expression of inner alignment.

Pace: The rhythm through which authority becomes visible.

Jurisdiction: Territory governed through agreement with truth.

Preemption: Disorder dissolving before it forms.

Use the words simply.
They point — they do not create.

Appendix B // Pattern Review

Daily Noticing

- Where did stillness remain without effort?
- Where did timing lead the interaction?
- Where did pressure dissolve on its own?
- Where did atmosphere settle before speech?
- Where did peace remain uninterrupted?

  Do not measure progress.
  Only notice continuity.

Occasional Reflection

- What environments now stabilize naturally?
- What reactions no longer appear?
- Where is speech no longer necessary?
- What resolves before I intervene?

Appendix C // Scripture on Authority & Peace

Stillness

- *"Be still, and know that I am God."* — Psalm 46:10

- *"He opened not His mouth."* — Isaiah 53:7

Voice

- *"Peace, be still."* — Mark 4:39

- *"My sheep hear My voice."* — John 10:27

Authority

- *"All authority... has been given to Me."* — Matthew 28:18

- *"Whatever you bind on earth..."* — Matthew 18:18

Knowing

- *"He knew their thoughts."* — Luke 6:8

Dominion // The Ground Beneath the Path

Dominion is not exerted.
It is recognized.

Given

- *"Let them have dominion..."* — Genesis 1:26

Restored

- *"I give you authority..."* — Luke 10:19

Lived

- *"My peace I give to you."* — John 14:27
  **Peace is no longer practiced.
  Peace remains.**

Remain.

Nothing needs to be restarted.
Nothing needs to be rehearsed.

What settled remains settled.
What aligned remains aligned.

Peace is no longer practiced.
It abides.

If the signal held,
the manual continues:

thealignmentarchive.com/manual

About the Author

Anna is the founder of *The Alignment Archive* and publisher of *The Alignment Press*.

Her work explores presence, restraint, and disciplined formation through lived practice rather than performance.

The Alignment Archive is a body of work devoted to containment, authority, and the quiet mechanics of alignment.

thealignmentarchive.com

www.ingramcontent.com/pod-product-compliance
Lightning Source LLC
Chambersburg PA
CBHW020456160726
47991CB00007B/2681